Arsen Blink

MAKE MONEY ONLINE

ARSEN BLINK

MAKE MONEY ONLINE

1.   HAVE A FRESH START

How many articles are there about making money online? Thousands? Millions? Enough? Probably. But there's a problem. Too many of them are just sales pitches to convince you to sign up for some seminar, webinar, training session or some other way to become an online millionaire.

They really give online money making a bad name. But it is possible to make money online. I mean, the people selling all of those millionaire pitches are making money, right?

There are legitimate ways to make money online. The problem is that the real ways to make money aren't "get rich quick" schemes.

Most of them require a lot of work and sometimes a lot of dedication before seeing a return on your time. But if you really want to make money online, work from home or turn an idea into a business, you *can* do it. You can even earn money with apps if you don't want to venture all the way to the computer.

I'm going to tell you about all kinds of legitimate ways to make money online. Since we are talking about *legitimate* jobs, you've got to be…well, legitimate. And no, you don't have to give everything up to have a fresh start.

Many of these options are *real* jobs that require you to put in hours if you want to get paid. They also require *real* work. Here are some tips for actually getting the job:

- **Take it seriously.** Yes, you're applying for an online job. Yes, you can do the work in your underwear, but that doesn't mean it's not a "real job". You must treat it as such or they aren't going to treat you as a serious candidate. You aren't the only one who wants to work in their underwear. In fact, the competition online is likely higher than it is in your local area.

- **Be professional.** When you submit a résumé, don't type it in ALL CAPS and please don't avoid the caps lock like the plague. Know how to use it without looking incompetent. Write in complete sentences with proper grammar. Of course, there will be exceptions, but even with the exceptions, you must keep it professional. You're building their view of you.

- **Give some, but not all.** Whether you're providing writing samples, a photography portfolio or links to your work, give them enough examples to get the idea, but not so many that they don't even know where to start. And while we're on the topic, give them some of your background information, but don't tell them your life story.

- **Double check yourself**, before you double wreck yourself. Make sure everything you send to a company, whether a résumé, an email or a portfolio, is good to go. Double check your grammar and wording, and for God's sake use spell check! This is especially important when it comes to the company's name. Don't spell their name wrong and be sure to type it how they type it (e.g. Problogger, not Pro Blogger).

Below are 35 ways to make money online organized into categories (with unique tips to make each way work) :

Websites

Let's go ahead and get this out of the way. There are all kinds of websites that will pay you for various things, such as shopping, taking surveys or testing products. No, I'm not getting paid to promote any of these and no, these websites won't make you a millionaire, but they are great for earning some extra cash. I'll leave out the scams.

Here are some legitimate websites that pay:

1. Swagbucks – Swagbucks is great for earning some extra cash. You can do a variety of things to make money, from taking surveys to using their search engine. You won't get rich, but you will earn a few bucks. If you have the time to kill, you can spend it earning some extra cash, instead of surfing the web.

2. InboxDollars – InboxDollars is similar to Swagbucks, since you're going to be taking surveys, shopping, etc., so if you want to maximize your return, sign up with both websites. They also offer a search engine that pays you (like Swagbucks) and you get $5 just for signing up. I won't continue to list survey sites one after another down the list, but if you want to get paid to take surveys, also check out GlobalTestMarket, E-Poll Surveys and Survey Club.

3. Project Payday
– Project Payday is one of those sites that has testimonials of people who have earned thousands of dollars by getting paid to get trial offers. I'm not saying you'll earn thousands, but it is legit and you can earn some extra cash. They assume that by paying you to do a free trial, you'll either like the product and purchase it, or forget to cancel the trial and get charged for it. If you can keep track and cancel before you get charged (if you don't want the product), then this is a great site for making some money.

4. User Testing – User Testing pays $10 a pop for testing websites. A test usually takes about 15-20 minutes. The purpose is for a website owner to watch someone, who is new to their site, try to navigate it. The value that the site owner gets by watching an actual user experience is worth a ton, but $10 isn't a bad pay-out.

5. Fiverr – Fiverr is a great place to make a few bucks or spend a few bucks if you need some of the services people offer. Basically, everything is $5. You either pay $5 or charge $5. They call them "gigs." You can offer your services however you choose. If you sell art and you're fine selling pieces for $5 each, that's a gig. If you're a graphic designer and you want to offer your services for $10/hour, simply offer a 30 minute gig. If they need two hours of graphic design, they pay you $20, or $10/hour by buying four gigs.

1. **IZEA** – IZEA works in addition to a blog or on its own. You get paid to blog, tweet, take photos and take videos. The pay is mostly based on your following, so if you want to make money with your tweets, you'll need to grow you Twitter following. Likewise, if you want to make money with blogs, you'll need substantial blog traffic (more on blogging below).

Freelance Writing

Freelance writing is one of the most popular ways to earn money online. Many successful freelancers can earn an average of 50 cents to a dollar per word. Some are earning twice that!

Of course, it doesn't start out like that. You've got to build your portfolio and your résumé, blah blah blah. If you're interested in writing, I'm sure you know this. If you're not interested in writing, I wouldn't recommend traveling down this road just for the money. It takes dedication and time, though it can be highly profitable if it's what you love. Assuming it is what you love, let's talk about making money with it.

Before you decide to start reaching out to all of these freelance writing companies, you need to have a web presence. You need a blog (in my humble blogger opinion, of course).

Or you could just have an online portfolio. Even a LinkedIn profile works to get started. When you're ready to start, here are 150 resources to help you write better, faster and more persuasively.

If that's intimidating, just start with these 50 resources.

Now for what you've all been waiting for; once you're ready to actually start making money, here are 10 websites you can start with:

7. Listverse – Listverse pays $100 for each accepted post. The article must be a list, it must be at least 1,500 words and you must include at least 10 things. Other than that, you can get pretty creative with it.

8. TopTenz – TopTenz pays $50 for each accepted post. Again, the article has to be in a list format and it must be at least 1,500 words, with few exceptions. They post often so your chances of getting accepted are fairly high.

9. A List Apart – A List Apart pays $200 for each accepted post. They're not first on the list, because they tend to publish less articles, which means you have a smaller chance of getting accepted. Same guidelines as above, 1,500 word minimum.

10. International Living – International Living pays $75 for each accepted post. They are mostly looking for travel experiences from countries you have visited. For this site, it's more about your experience than your writing ability.

11. FundsforWriters – FundsforWriters pays $50 for each accepted post. They are looking for articles about writing and making money with it. They only accept articles between 500-600 words, but they want you to make each word count.

12. Uxbooth – Uxbooth pays $100 for each accepted post. They do tend to take four to eight weeks to accept and post articles, so don't count on this being a quick money maker. They take so long, because they pair with editors to only publish amazing content.

13. iWriter – iWriter pays up to $15 for each accepted post. That may seem small, but they aren't as strict as many of the others above and they also allow you to pick exactly what you write. You can write as many or as few articles as you want.

14. Textbroker – Textbroker pays up to five cents per word, if you're a 5-star writer. You'll start by submitting a short sample article and you will most likely start as a 3-star writer, but you can work your way up by writing more and writing great content.

15. Matador Network – Matador Network pays up to $60 for each accepted post, but standard pay is around $20-$25. They don't really focus on a minimum word count, but they have a maximum count of 1,500 words.

16. The Penny Hoarder – The Penny Hoarder pays up to $800 (rarely), depending upon the number of page views you receive.

The pay starts at $100 for 50,000 page views, so this isn't a guaranteed paid article, but it can potentially be highly rewarding.

There's no doubt that you can make money with freelance writing, but it's a process. Once you start building your portfolio and your writing skills, you can start making some serious money. If you're not an experienced writer, expect to put some time in before you really start to see some dough.

Sell

Ever since the idea of online auctions came into existence, the online selling market has been on the rise. Many are interested, but don't know how to get started. There are still all kinds of ways to make money by selling online, whether you're selling what you already have or buying and selling like a store. Before we get started, here are a few general tips when selling anything online:

- **Get a PayPal account.** If you don't have a PayPal account, you'll want to get one if you're doing business online. It's the standard in online business for receiving payment and paying others.

- **Take good pictures.** Some of the options below don't require you to actually take the picture and sell the product, but for the ones that do, make sure you take a clear picture that makes your product stand out from the others. If you're going to be taking a lot of pictures, set up a small "studio-like" area in your home with a backdrop and proper lighting to really make your pictures come across as professional. And of course, you'll want a good camera too.

- **Be honest.** If you're selling used items, be honest about every dent, scratch, blemish, etc.. This will reduce many issues you could run into and keep your reviews positive.

- **Do good business.** Plain and simple. Whether you're selling on a small site or opening an online store, your customer service matters. You'll want to get those positive reviews and make a good name for yourself. Respond to questions, concerns and complaints. Offer a guarantee if available.

Follow those guidelines and you will do well in online sales. When you're ready to start selling, here's where you go:

17. Amazon – Have you heard of FBA? It stands for "Fulfilled by Amazon" and it's getting pretty popular. Basically, you buy products (in bulk is best) and ship them to Amazon for them to store. When your products sell, Amazon packs them up, ships them out and sends you the money (after taking their cut). There are people making a full-time living from FBA, while others just do it for some extra money.

18. CraigsList – Some things don't ship very well. Other things may make you feel uncomfortable to sell to someone across the country. Anytime you're selling a large item or something you just don't want to ship, Craigslist is a great place to go. It's simple to list your item (again, take good pictures!). If you don't like the idea of putting your phone number out there, the interested individual can send you a message to your inbox without even getting your email address.

19. eBay – Of course you can't read an article about making money online that doesn't mention eBay. You can start an eBay store and get serious about it or you can just sell some stuff to declutter your home. Either way, I've made my fair share from selling on eBay and it's still a popular way to earn money. If you decide to start an actual eBay store, you'll want to find a drop-ship business like Doba that will store and ship items straight to your customers so you don't have to deal with an inventory.

20. Etsy – If you like to create arts and crafts, you can sell them on Etsy.It's completely free to open an Etsy store. You simply sign up, post pictures of your creations and starting selling. You can choose your payment option, but PayPal is generally the easiest. Etsy makes it easy to sell and keep track of your inventory. There is a small listing fee and they take 3.5% of every sale you make.

21. Facebook – Facebook swap shops are great for selling things locally. It's like CraigsList, but a little easier. You simply search for swap shops in your area and ask to join the group. Once you're in, take a picture of the item, write a quick description with the price and post it. It doesn't get much easier than that. You can generally expect to get about what you would get at a yard sale, maybe a little more.

Blogging

Hey look, an article about making money online that doesn't mention blogging. . . oh wait, here it is.

First off, I'm a blogger so it seems wrong not to mention it, but more importantly, it's a legitimate way to make money. It's quite possibly the least straight-forward way on this list, but it's very doable and it's also quite possibly the funnest way on this list. I love blogging and I know hundreds of bloggers who feel the same. So let's talk about making money blogging and what it really means.

Blogging is something that requires patience, persistence and discipline. It may mean writing everyday for over a year before you really start to see any money from it. There are exceptions to the rule, but from my dealings with other bloggers, it seems to be pretty common to spend one or even two years building your blog, your brand and your authority, before making any serious amount of money.

Some people argue that you can make money without a lot of traffic and while that is true in some circumstances, you will generally need a lot of website traffic to start earning from a blog and that takes a while. Once you've reached that point, here are the primary ways to monetize your blog and start earning:

22. Advertising – This is definitely the most old-school way of earning money with a blog. It's also starting to become the least common way. You can sell advertising spots directly on your site or you can sign up with a company like Google AdSense or Media.net. Either way, you won't see a whole lot of money from ads until your views are well into the thousands each day.

23. Affiliates – There are many affiliate networks, such as FlexOffers and CJ Affiliate that allow you to promote other people's products and services. You simply put a link or a banner on your page and then you get a percentage if someone clicks through and buys the product/service. You'll want to select products that are specifically within your blog's category.This is an effective way to earn money once you have the traffic coming to your blog.

24. Membership – Many people have created a paid membership area on their blog. This is typically for exclusive content that you can only access in the "member's area." If you have a really great idea on what to include, this can be a great idea. You'll have to create something that can't easily be accessed around the web.

25. Products – You can create your own product, such as an ebook or computer software. You would then use your blog as a promotion tool to get people to buy your product. As long as you create a legitimate product with a whole lot of value, you should be able to get some buyers, but like everything else with a blog, you'll need the traffic to get the sells.

26. Services – You can offer a paid service, such as life coaching, blog coaching, goal setting or financial planning. Just be sure to investigate all the legal implications and make sure you're not claiming to be a professional if you're not one. With a service like this, you're basically using your blog to sell yourself. You'll need to convince people that you're worth buying and then be able to back up your claims once they purchase your service.

27. Sponsored/paid posts – Many blogs publish sponsored and paid posts. Sponsored posts are basically just posts about a specific brand, product or service. A company will pay you to publish an article about it. It's similar with other paid posts as well. Your basically selling the spot for the article on your site. If you decide to take this route, you'll want to build your traffic before you will get many offers.

28. Subscription – If you think of something valuable (newsletter, online magazine, etc.) that you can consistently offer on a certain basis (weekly, monthly, etc.), you may want to offer a subscription service. This could be a fee charged each time your product is sent out or on a monthly basis. Either way, this has to be something that your customers can only get by subscribing to your website.

29. Videos – This could be an entire section on it's own. Many people have made money by creating YouTube videos. Evan of EvanTube is a kid and he has made millions by creating reviews of products that other kids his age would use. It's not easy to get views into the millions, but once you do, you'll start seeing some cash come in. Many bloggers have completely turned to videos to get their point across by starting a video blog.
If you're truly interested in becoming a blogger, start by looking through the archives of ProBlogger, Copyblogger and Boost Blog Traffic. Then go read through all the free guides over at Quick Sprout. It may take you a year to complete those tasks alone, but it will be worth it. You'll practically have a MBA in blogging.

Work-at-Home Companies

Finally, there are some companies that will hire you to work from the comfort of your own home. If you're interested in working for someone else, while still making your own schedule and deciding where to work from, here are a few companies that will let you do just that:

30. CrowdSource – CrowdSource offers many types of jobs from "microtask" jobs to larger writing and editing jobs. You decide how much you work and you can do most of it right at your computer.

31. Demand Studios – Demand Studios is hiring all kinds of creative professionals, from writer to filmmakers. The pay isn't amazing, but it's competitive for a work-at-home job.

32. Fast Chart – Fast Chart allows you to work from home as a medical transcriptionist. There are some requirments and qualifications listed on the page, but if you meet them, you'll make competitive pay for the industry. You'll also be able to set your own schedule since you'll be working from home.

33. Leap Force – Leap Force is one way that Google rates websites for search engine ranking. If you're hired, you make decent money (usually over $11/hour), you set your own schedule and it can be pretty fun to view and rank websites.

34. Liveops – Liveops is a call center that allows you to work from home. Once your set up to take the calls, you can begin making a weekly schedule and working from home. The pay is generally close to $10/hour, but you can earn more with commissions.

35. SpeakWrite – SpeakWrite will pay you up to $15/hour to transcribe information. You set your own schedule and work from home.

Now you've got many different options to start earning online. If you saw something that really interests you, try it out and learn more about it. If you're really wanting to make a full-time income online, you need to be dedicated to learning how to do what you want to do. There are tons of free resources out there. You just have to search for them!

Need Motivation to Get What You Want?
No matter what sort of challenges you're facing, you'll probably need loads of motivation. So don't miss this valuable guide to give you a motivation boost!

You need quality products :

Improve your customer retention, build brand trust and boost your ROI by focusing on your product quality. Tips ahead!
Quality is what a product can do for a customer.

Product quality is also how well the product does what it's supposed to do, and how well it holds up over time. Some consumers view quality as a price point while others appreciate a product because it's "greener."
Regardless of the various viewpoints from the public, product quality is a competitive marker for brands that affects purchasing decisions and profitability.

Brands and marketers can't afford to overlook product quality for the following five reasons.

Related Article: Under Promise, Over Deliver: The Must-Do's of Customer Retention

Marketing studies have proved again and again that high-quality brands will obtain more repeat purchases. Spending more time and money upfront perfecting a product before it hits the market will minimize customer complaints and returns.

It's common for sellers of high-quality brands to spend more to persuade consumers to try their goods since the present value of a trial purchase is larger. The more successful companies are at pleasing customers during their initial experience with a product, the more likely they'll be to see repeat purchases from those same people.

One dimension of quality is how a product looks, feels, sounds, tastes or smells. For example, MrTakeOutBags pays close attention to aesthetics, and it shows in their bakery cupcake boxes.

The colors, prints, shapes, textures and features (such as handles) make all the difference, and it's what sets them apart from the competition. Customers notice this kind of details, and they can make or break a sale. There are so many similar product options out there these days that unique attributes and designs have a big impact on purchasing decisions.

Bonus

Many families prefer the flexibility of using an online tutor. Depending on your background, you could be simply helping a child with homework or providing college-level support. You need to have your own computer and high speed internet. Experience required differs among companies. Some require "strong experience," while others require a specific educational background. However, most companies do require a college degree.

- Some companies assign students to you, while others post your profile on their site and let custumers select you.
-
- You can make anywhere from $9 to $30 per hour based on your educational background and the subject you teach.

- Sites that hire elementary-level tutors include Tutor.com, HomeworkHelp.com, Aim4a and Brainfus e.

- Kaplan hires SAT and ACT tutors.

You can also :

Create content that people will find valuable and that will help you rank higher in the search engines. Keyword research can help you to find out what topics people are searching. Write content on these topics to improve your rank in the search engines. You cannot monetize without any visitors.

- Use a tool like Market Samurai to do keyword research.

- Put out advertisements to increase traffic to your site.

- Create a marketing campaign using social media outlets such as Facebook or Twitter.

If you take the time to reflect on your experiences, you will realize that you have more knowledge about which to write than you might think. Begin by listing three assets that define you, such as your profession, a special hobby or a personality trait.

Next, list three things that inspire you, such as religion, education or charity. Finally, list three of your dreams, such as getting married, traveling or spending more time with your children. These three lists should give you many ideas of topics about which you can write.

As a freelance writer, much of your work will likely be published on the internet. The principles of writing for the web differ slightly than writing for print. The content must still be high-quality and well-written, but the presentation must be adjusted for the way people read online material.

- Because of the low resolution of online text, readers tend to scan rather than read everything from top to bottom. Make your text easily scannable by breaking up text using descriptive headings and bullet points.

- Get to the point by using the inverted pyramid style. This means writing the conclusion first and then providing examples to support it.

- Make your copy effective by being concise and using simple language. Aim your writing to an eighth-grade reading level. Remove unnecessary or confusing words or terms.

- Include keywords and phrases that improve your ranking in the search engines.[18]

When you first start out, you may have to accept work writing about a topic you don't find all that interesting. You must keep an open mind and be willing to accept work that may not be in your desired field. However, as you continue to write, you not only learn about more topics, but you also build your reputation. With time, you can be choosier about assignments you want to accept.

- Browse the internet for freelancing websites that hire people to do work online.

When you first start out as a freelance writer, it can be hard to get work without any published samples. However, it is possible to get quality samples if you are willing to do some writing for free. First, you can publish content on your own blog or website. Also, you can write guest posts for someone else's blog. Finally, you can write blog posts for free in exchange for a byline.

2 HOW TO MAKE MONEY ON AMAZON

1. Amazon Associates

As a blogger, I love the Amazon affiliate program. As an affiliate, aka Associate, you earn a commission on every sale you refer to the site. While many complain the rates are low, they do offer a progressive earnings structure on most general merchandise. The more you sell, the more you earn – from 4% to 8.5%. Amazon also has several "Bounty" opportunities where you can earn a set fee of $3 to $25 for referring people to sign up for Prime, Amazon Student, Audible, Baby & Wedding Registries and more.

Chris Guthrie, Pot Pie Girl and Tiffany Dow are three people who really turned me on to the potential of the Amazon Associates program, where I've learned to increase my earnings year after year.

2. Amazon FBA

This year we spoke with Cynthia Stine who has been able to create a $40,000+ per year business in just ten hours per week selling things on Amazon. This seller opportunity eliminates the need to deal with shipping and returns. You send the stuff you want to sell to the Amazon warehouse, and they take care of the sales process.

That being said, product selection is key. Send in a bunch of stuff that never sells and you may end up paying storage fees. Luckily, The Selling Family has some really great courses that deal with every aspect of the FBA process including special holidays and category ungating.

3. Amazon Merch

This is a new vertical from Amazon that allows brands and creatives to upload their designs to the site to be sold as t-shirts. There is very little risk involved with this type of sales model as no upfront payment is required, but competition can be high and you will likely need to invest some money into advertising if you don't have a large following of your own. This opportunity has been so popular that you will need to request an invitation at this time.

4. Amazon Handmade

This new vertical was touted as an alternative to Etsy. As a seller, Amazon allows you to sell your handmade wares on the site. In some instances, you can even have them listed as Prime and FBA items. The reviews on Handmade are mixed. Apparently "handmade" items don't need to meet the stringent requirements of Etsy. There also isn't the one-on-one customer support aspect that comes with Etsy. Amazon is largely a mass retailer connecting individual buyers and sellers that may never cross paths again. That isn't going away with Handmade.

5. Amazon Mechanical Turk

Mechanical Turk, or mTurk, isn't necessarily what I would consider one of the best ways to make money on Amazon, but it is a way nonetheless. This crowdsourcing site has been around since before I started working from home in 2007 and allows workers to earn money completing small tasks. The majority of the things I did here back in the day were transcription, data entry, categorizing. It's often mindless work that takes only a few minutes to complete. The pay reflects that. You aren't going to make a livable wage on mTurk, but it can be a fun way to pass the time if nothing good is on television.

6. Amazon Kindle

For so very long, Amazon Kindle was the way to go if you wanted to self-publish an ebook. There are no upfront fees involved. Amazon simply takes a cut of each sale; you get 35% to 70% depending on the listing. Since Amazon owns CreateSpace, you can make printed copies available as well.

Self-publishing isn't as difficult as it sounds. You can handle much of the process yourself and outsource editing and design on Fiverr.

7. Amazon Trade-In

The Amazon Trade-In program doesn't offer cash, but they do pay you in gift cards for select used books, video games and electronics. One thing I really like as an Amazon customer is that they will let me know when something I have bought on Amazon has a trade-in value. On the day I wrote this post, I was able to trade-in one of my books for $6.04. And I did! I was done with the book. It wasn't one I took notes in. I shop on Amazon a lot. I can use that store credit.

You have an Amazon Gift Card value of up to $6.04

Add or remove suggested items from your Trade-In list that you bought from Amazon or elsewhere.

Get up to $6.04

No trade-in offer available

8. Amazon Flex

Same-day delivery is hot right now. We don't want to wait for anything these days! Amazon is just starting to roll out same-day delivery in select metropolitan areas. Flex will allow them to take advantage of the availability of people just like you to make those deliveries.

You will need a car, smartphone and Amazon account to make Flex deliveries. The company is currently stating pay of $18 to $25 per hour with a big emphasis on flexibility and availability of hours.

9. Amazon At-Home Customer Service

Amazon is one of the many online retailers that employs a virtual workforce. As an Amazon Work-from-Home Customer Service Associate you will earn a base pay of $10 per hour. Full-time and part-time opportunities are available in Arizona, Kentucky, Texas, West Virginia, Delaware, Minnesota, Florida, Georgia, Kansas,

North Carolina, Tennessee, Wisconsin, and Virginia. These positions are largely seasonal with the potential to become permanent.

10. CamperForce

If you're an avid RV'er with a mobile lifestyle, Amazon CamperForce could be a great opportunity for you to make some money! Amazon will pay your campsite fees (plus most utilities) if you travel to their designated campground to work for the holiday season – from early Fall through December 23. As a member of Amazon's CamperForce, you will spend three or four months picking, packing, stowing, and receiving orders and merchandise. They don't advertise their pay, but do state that they're "good wages" and you receive a shift differential depending on which shift you work. If you work overtime, you'll be paid time and a half; you can also earn a completion bonus by working the full season through to December 23. That's all in addition to having most of your living costs paid! And you can earn referral bonuses as well.

11. Amazon Vine

This one isn't an actual exchange of cash but rather goods. Amazon's most trusted reviewers are invited to Vine Voices program and have the opportunity to receive free product in exchange for leaving a review on the site. This is an invite-only program offered to those who leave frequent reviews that are found most helpful by the Amazon community.

12. Amazon Services

Amazon has their hand in every pie these days including the local service market! If you offer professional services like handyman, housecleaning and more, you may be able to get an invite to the exclusive Amazon Services community. There are no upfront fees. Instead, Amazon takes a 15-20% cut when they refer customers to you.

13. Amazon Influencers

I'm a big fan of the new Amazon Influencers program. You don't need a blog or website for this affiliate opportunity, only an engaged following on Twitter, YouTube, Facebook and or Instagram. Once approved, you will be provided with a virtual storefront in which you can add your favorite products from Amazon. Then, you can easily share your Influencer Page on social media with your new vanity URL. (Ex. Mine is https://www.amazon.com/shop/angienelson.) You can then earn commission on qualified product sales once someone clicks visits your store.

The commission rates are said to be similar to Amazon Associates. And if you have an Associates account, this two can link up for easy reporting. There are some great features with Influencers that aren't available through the Associates program:

- You can share your Page URL within emails (Yay!)
- Fashion Influencers may be able to get product gifts, sponsorships and more.
- You can share Amazon coupon codes on social media
- and more

This program isn't available to everyone, but if you have a strong social media following it's worth a shot! Apply here.

Those are a few of my favorite ways to make money on Amazon. I'd love to hear how you have profited from the site.

15 Ways to Make Money on Amazon

It's hard to believe **Amazon** started off as a small website selling used books. The world's largest retailer, with now **worth over $602 billion**, continues to grow exponentially, and some financial experts predict the company will soon be worth $1 trillion.

Amazon isn't just your go-to place for online shopping, the company also produces TV shows and movies through Amazon Studios, and for $13 billion, claimed their stake in the grocery business with their purchase of Whole Foods in 2017. Amazon also owns Zappos, IMBD, Audible, Goodreads, and Twitch.tv, to name a few.

As the company grows, so has its marketplace for sellers, and because the company offers so many different services and products, they're able to carve out unique jobs and side hustles for people who want to earn extra money, work from home, and of course, become a seller.

If you're ready for to explore ways to make money with Amazon, these are some of your best options.

1. Sell a product using Amazon's FBA

FBA means **fulfilled by Amazon**, and as a seller, all you would need to do is ship your inventory of products to Amazon's warehouse and they take care of shipping it for you.

Some merchants choose to ship out products themselves, in order to avoid hefty fees Amazon charges. There are pros and cons of doing this, but if your product sells in high volume, it makes the most sense to ship via FBA.

Out of all the options listed in this article about ways to make money with Amazon, becoming a seller has the greatest opportunity for you to cash in on extra income, but it also involves the most amount of research and uncertainty.

Selling a product on Amazon can be a great way to earn some extra income, but don't start selling without first understanding what it entails. You run the risk of losing money if you don't do your due diligence first. I'm speaking from first-hand experience on that one.

My Amazon Mistake

I've sold products on Amazon for the last year, and I've learned that research is a critical factor, before you start.

This was my biggest mistake. In a nutshell, I didn't do enough research around the product before making a huge purchase of 1,000 units. After shipping costs from China were factored into the retail price, the product ended up being too expensive to sell (based on competitors' prices), and I was forced to take a loss.

If you want to really learn about how to sell on Amazon, it takes a lot of due diligence, YouTubing, reading and talking to others who have been in the business.

The awesome thing about Amazon is the sheer number of potential customers that may click and hopefully buy your item. The downside is, you face fierce competition by other sellers who are doing the exact same thing as you.

However, the opportunity is still there, and I'm here to tell you that it's possible to sell on Amazon and make money.

What to understand, before you sell

The competition to sell a product on Amazon is high. Who knows if the product you choose to sell will even sell? It's a bit of a gamble, but once you figure out Amazon's rules and oddities, it can be very lucrative, particularly around the holidays.

Let's say, after doing your product research on Amazon, you want to sell an olive oil dispenser that you can easily source from Alibaba. Most likely, you won't be the first person selling this item – not to say that you have to be the first or only person to sell something to be successful.

However, if you do start selling a high volume of them, chances are, another seller will see that and follow suit.

Something else to note is that many categories of items require approval from Amazon before you start selling. It's called getting "ungated."

Examples of products that need approval from Amazon first include groceries, jewelry and beauty, to name a few.

The process around getting ungated for a product category is hazy, at best. You have to send Amazon invoices for the items you purchased and intend to sell. For the first time seller, it can be a Catch-22 because you're expected to have proof of enough inventory, but you may not get approved to sell.

At one point, I tried to sell grocery products and kept getting rejected from Amazon, without any reason why.

Because Amazon is such a huge corporation, talking to a real human often involves getting the runaround from overseas customer service agents who simply read from a script and aren't very helpful. It's just one of the many frustrations that come with huge companies, like Amazon.

Once you get approved and start selling, you won't have to dedicate quite so many hours to maintaining the business. In my case, after we were approved to sell our item, we packaged and shipped the items to Amazon's warehouse with individual barcode stickers on them.

5 Things I've Learned As a Seller

Now that I've had the business for about a year, these are my biggest takeaways:

- Sell an item that's in the $30-50 range, and aim for margins to be $20, if possible.
- Make sure you have plenty of inventory at least 3-6 months before the holidays. Stock up, because your sales will (hopefully) ride the holiday wave.
- If you're sourcing from China, be aware that China has a lot of holidays, especially Chinese New Year. Basically, this means China is shut down for about a month some time between February and March.
- Make sure you're calculating Amazon's fees carefully. Amazon's cut is significant, from shipping fees to your seller's subscription. There are lots of calculators that Amazon sellers have created, to help bring some transparency around how much fees cost a seller, so you can accurately calculate revenue.
- Similar to number four, calculate your shipping fees carefully too. If you're sourcing from China, understand how the shipping costs will eat into your bottom line.

A friend of mine was able to find a source for a product he was selling, literally in the next city over from where he lived. This meant his bottom line was higher because he was able to avoid international shipping costs.

2. Private Label Your Product

In order to avoid some of the competition on Amazon, many sellers have opted to private label their item, which means they are registering it on Amazon as their own.

The process for private labeling is more complicated than simply buying an item from Alibaba and selling it.

The upside to selling your own branded product on Amazon is that you always have full control for your listing and you can make changes to your product, if you need to. Let's say your customers complained about a particular feature of your product, you could then make modifications to it.

For example, let's say you sold pencils, but noticed a lot of the negative reviews mentioned that they wished the eraser worked better, and that the pencil itself was wider, for better grip. You can then take those recommendations from reviewers and craft your own pencil and get it trademarked.

Check out **this guide on how to sell on amazon** from a 7 figure seller!

3. Retail Arbitrage

This is the opposite of private labeling. **Retail arbitrage** simply means buying low and selling high. Some sellers make their entire living on just retail arbitrage and have carved out a lucrative niche for themselves.

A lot of sellers who do retail arbitrage try to avoid the cost of shipping (i.e. shipping from China is very expensive and eats into your profits), so they simply drive directly to the location and load up on cheap items they think will sell.

Therefore, many sellers spend a lot of time cruising through their local Walmarts to find the best and cheapest deals on just about anything. They buy up as many items that are on clearance and then sell it on Amazon.

I heard a podcast on Side Hustle Nation where a couple made their full-time living on retail arbitrage on Amazon and made over a million dollars in sales every year.

Their strategy was pretty simple. Check out their local Walmarts and use an app to scan items to see how much it's selling for on Amazon. (Here is a useful comparison of **two of the best scanning apps** Amazon sellers use.) Then, they use their knowledge of what's been successful in the past to decide whether they think it'll be a product worth selling.

This couple went to the Walmarts near their home so often that they knew all the sales managers and would often be given a discount for buying up all of the video games, which sometimes involved purchasing hundreds of them at a time.

Retail arbitrage isn't for everyone, because it involves a lot of research and time to find places that are having crazy liquidation and clearance sales (there are even sites you can subscribe to that will give you the inside scoop on where to go for the cheapest liquidation sales), plus it will most likely involve driving to the retail location to pick up the items.

4. Work As a Delivery Fulfilment Warehouse Associate

If you're in the proper location, you can apply to be a **delivery warehouse associate** for their fulfillment centers, sortation centers, delivery stations, Prime Now locations, Campus Pickup Points and customer service centers.

You can filter your search by full or part-time positions and by location.

5. Amazon Flex

Sometimes when I order from Amazon, I notice plain-clothed delivery associates delivering my packages.

Amazon's same-day delivery option for customers has sparked a need for more delivery help in various metropolitan areas. If you have a reliable car and a smartphone, consider delivering goods through Amazon Prime.

The company currently pays anywhere from $18-25 per hour and you need to download the app and answer a few simple questions before you can **get started**. They emphasize flexibility and availability of shifts, but the downside is there aren't always opportunities in your area.

I have a friend who does this to earn extra income, and he says he often finishes his shift a few hours early, but still gets paid for the entire five hours, or pre-set hours.

Of course, this may not be true for everyone who delivers for Amazon, but it's a nice to know you can finish early but still get compensated for the agreed upon time.

6. Work from Home for Amazon

If you want a job where you can be **home-based**, consider a spot on Amazon's virtual **customer service team**, also known as Amazon's Work-from-Home Customer Service Associate.

Virtual opportunities aren't available everywhere but If you live in a certain area, you may be able to apply for Amazon's "work-from-home" positions, given that you're qualified and a right fit for the position.

The base pay is $10 an hour and full and part-time positions are only available in certain areas, however, you can filter your search by the work-from-home category and by location.

This is more of a seasonal position but has the potential to become a permanent.

There were all kinds of positions listed, such as customer service rep positions for those who speak a second language, other than English.

There are also non-customers service positions that those with a qualified tech background could potentially apply for, such as cloud tech account managers and technical trainer.

7. Become an Amazon Affiliate, Amazon Associates

3 HOW TO MAKE MONEY BLOGGING.

I'm often asked how to make money blogging so want in this article to lay out some basic steps that I see most bloggers who make a living from blogging go through.

Here is how to make money from a blog:

1. Set up your blog

2. Start creating useful content

3. Get off your blog and start finding readers

4. Build engagement with the readers that come

5. Start making money from the readership you have through one or more of a variety of income streams

Sounds easy doesn't it! On some levels the process is simple – but you need to know up front that there's a lot to each step and below I'm going to give you some pointers on each including some further reading.

Here's how to make money from a blog.

1. Start a Blog

In order to make money blogging you're going to need to have a blog. While this is pretty obvious it is also a stumbling block for many PreBloggers who come to the idea of blogging with little or no technical background.

If that's you – don't worry! It was my story too and most bloggers start out feeling a little overwhelmed by the process of starting their blog.

If you need a little help I would highly recommend you check out my article **How to Start a Blog** in which I run through the steps you need to take to get up and running. It's really not as hard as you might think!

Further Reading on starting a blog:

How to Start a Blog

2. Start Creating Useful Content

A blog is not a blog without content so once you've set your blog up you need to focus your attention upon creating useful content. What you choose to create will depend a little on the topic that you choose to write about (on that note, most successful bloggers have some focus to their blogging whether that be a **niche or a demographic** that they write for).

The key with creating content is to make it as useful as possible. Focus upon creating content that changes people's lives in some way will be the type of content that people will value the most and it will help people to feel like they know, like and trust you – which is really important if you later want to make money from your blog.

Further Reading on creating content:

There are thousands of articles and podcast episodes on ProBlogger about how to create content. See our latest stuff in the **content category on our blog** and on the **podcast**. Also check out some of these popular articles on different aspects of creating content.

- **How to Craft a Blog Post – 10 Crucial Points to Pause**
- **How to Create Blog Posts that People Remember**
- **The 4 Pillars of Writing Exceptional Blogs**
- How to Come Up With Fresh Ideas to Write About On Your Blog
- **11 Quick Tips for Writing Compelling Blog Posts**
- **How Often Should You Blog? (Hint: The Answer Might Surprise You)**
- **21 Ways to Write Posts that Are Guaranteed to Grow Your Blog**
- **10 Ways to Switch Your Brain to Writing Mode When Working From Home**

3. Get off your blog and start finding readers

As you create the most useful content that you possibly can it is easy to get very insular with your focus and spend most of your time looking at building your blog. Many bloggers have a 'build it and they will come mentality' with their blogging but this is a bit of a trap.

If you want to make money from your blog you need to not only focus upon building a great blog but it is also necessary to get off your blog and to start promoting it.

There are many ways to experiment with growing your blog's audience that I've written in previous blog posts and talked about in podcasts (I'll share some further reading and listening below) but it is important to enter into all these strategies remembering that you should not just be looking for 'traffic' but 'readers'.

Start by thinking carefully about the type of reader you'd like to have read your blog. You might like to create an **avatar of that reader** (sometimes called a reader persona or profile) to help you work out who you're trying to attract.

Once you know who you're hoping to have read your blog ask yourself where that type of person might already be gathering online. Begin to list where they might be gathering:

- Are they reading certain blogs? List the top 3

- Are they participating in certain forums? List the top 3

- Are they listening to podcasts? List the top 3

- Are they engaging on certain social networks? List the top 3

- Which accounts are they following on each of these social networks? List the top 3

Each of these places that you reader might already be gathering has opportunities to develop a presence whether that be by leaving good comments, offering to create guest posts or simply by being helpful and answering questions.

With this list of blogs, focus, podcasts, social media accounts in hand you will have some good spots to begin to hang out and create value.

The key is to build a presence, to add value, to foster relationships – not to engage in spammy practices.

Further Reading/Listening on the topic of Finding Readers for your Blog:

See our latest posts and podcasts on finding readers in the **finding readers section of the podcast** and **here on the blog**. Here are a few other links to check out on the topic:

- **5 Mistakes Bloggers Make with SEO and What To Do About Them**

- **Here's How My 2 Blogs Grew**

- **How to Socialize Your Posts for Maximum Effect**

- **How to Promote Yourself Without Coming Across as a Jerk**

- **11 Ways I Diversified Traffic Sources for My Blogs to Become Less Reliant Upon Google [With a Surprising Twist]**

- **Grow Traffic to Your Blog Through Guest Posting and Creating Content for Other Blogs, Forums, Media and Events**

- **2 Types of Content that Help You to Find Readers for Your Blog**

4. Build engagement with the readers that come

With sustained focus upon creating great content and finding readers for your blog you'll begin to notice people visiting your blog and engaging with your content.

At this point you need to switch your focus to engaging with those readers and building community.

Respond to comments, reach out to those readers personally and do everything that you can to keep them coming back again and again by **building a 'sticky blog'**.

Look after the readers you already have well and you'll find they spread the word of your blog for you and help make your blog even more widely read.

Having an engaged reader is also much easier to make money from.

Further Reading on deepening reader engagement on your blog:

•

○ **7 Strategies for Growing Community on Your Blog**

○ **11 Quick Tips to Get More Comments on Your Blog**

○ **Why You Should Make Building Community a Priority in Your Blogging**

5. Start making money from the readership you have through one or more of a variety of income streams

OK – the first four steps of starting a blog, creating content, finding readers and building engagement with those readers are important foundations that you really do need to get in place before you'll be able to build long term income for your blog.

There's no avoiding that what we've covered is a lot of work but if you do it well you'll be setting yourself up well and giving yourself every chance of being able to make money from your blog.

With these foundations in place you're now ready to start attempting to make money from your blog but you do need to be aware that just because you have set up your blog, have content and have engaged readers that the money won't just automatically flow.

It takes continued work and experimentation to make money from your blog.

I've written many articles here on ProBlogger on the topic of making money blogging and will link to some suggested further reading on the topic below but let me share a few introductory words on the topic first.

There are Many Ways to Make Money Blogging

One of the biggest misconceptions that I see bloggers having about monetising blogs is that they have to do it in one of a handful of ways. The reality is that there are many ways to make money from blogs.

A few years ago I decided to sit down and list all the ways that I saw bloggers making money from their blogs and created this 'money map' (click to enlarge).

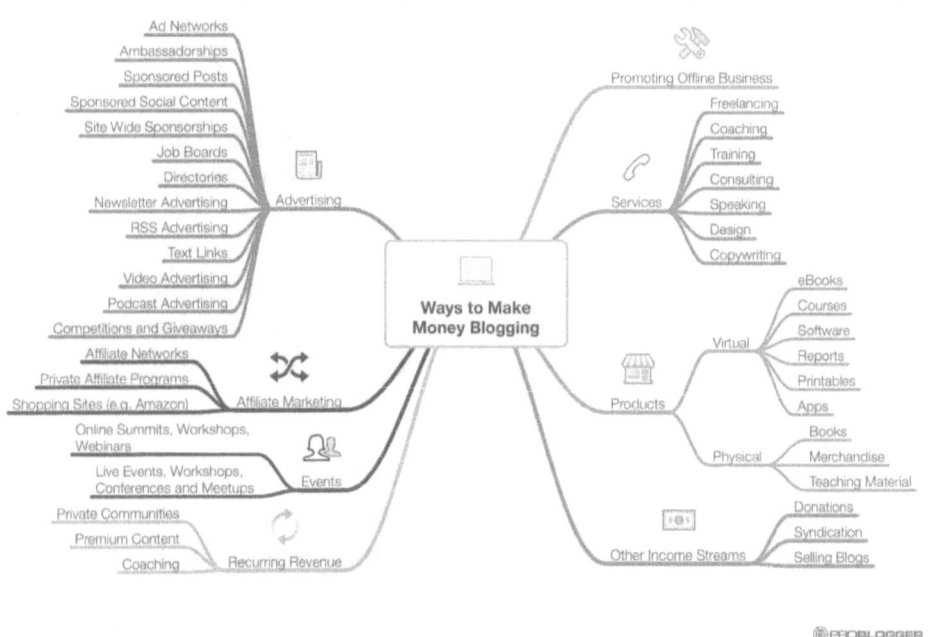

Note: this money map was updated in September 2016.

As you'll see there are quite a few options that bloggers have to derive income from their blogs.

Don't worry though – while this map is quite overwhelming at a first glance there are a few main 'clusters' of income streams that you might want to focus upon rather than all the specific ones.

1. Advertising Income

This is where many bloggers start. In many ways this model of making money from blogs is not dissimilar to how a magazine or newspaper sells ads. As your traffic and brand grows you'll find advertisers will be willing to pay to get exposure to your audience.

While you need decent traffic to do a direct deal with an advertisers there are ad networks (like Google AdSense) that act as a middleman and enable smaller publishers to run ads on their blogs. This is where many bloggers start (I did too).

2. Affiliate Income

A recent survey of ProBlogger readers found that affiliate promotions was the most common type of income that our readers have.

To put it most simply – affiliate income is when you link to a product that is for sale on another site (take Amazon for example) and if someone follows your link and ends up buying that product you earn a commission on that sale.

There's more to it than that but this is another great place to start with monetising your blog as affiliate programs are easy to sign up for and if you have an engaged audience you will find they follow the recommendations that you make on products.

Further reading on affiliate income:

- The Ultimate Guide to Making Money with the Amazon Affiliate Program
- 10 Popular Affiliate Programs for Small and Medium Sized Blogs

3. Events

While not something most bloggers do I have noticed an increase in the number of bloggers making money by running events.

These range from big conferences and events like our **ProBlogger Conference** which hosts hundreds of bloggers every year right down to smaller meet-ups for a blogger's readers where money is made either through charging readers to attend or by finding a sponsor for the event.

Alternatively online events or summits are getting more popular.

4. Recurring Income

Another growing category of income that I'm seeing more and more bloggers are experimenting is recurring income streams (sometimes called continuity programs or membership programs).

This is where readers pay a regular recurring amount (usually on a monthly or annual basis) for access to either premium content, a community area, some kind of service, tools, coaching (or some combination of these things).

6. Promoting a Business

Many brick and mortar businesses indirectly make money from their blogs by using their blogs to grow their profile and direct readers to their business.

7. Services

A common way that many bloggers make money is through offering services to their readers. These might be anything from coaching and consulting, to writing or copywriting, to design, training or other freelance services.

8. Products

While I started out making money from my blogs through advertising and affiliate promotions today my #1 source of income is through selling eBooks and courses on my blogs. These 'virtual products' take work to create but have been lucrative for me and many other bloggers.

Products can of course take many forms and income virtual information products like eBooks or courses but also other virtual products like software, reports etc.

The other type of product some bloggers sell is physical products. This is most common when the blogger has a business but sometimes bloggers also create merchandise (T-shirts etc) or other physical products to sell.

Other Income Streams

There are of course other forms of income that bloggers experiment with. Some include asking for donations, syndicating content to other sites and lastly selling their blogs.

Multiple Income Streams

Most full time bloggers make money more than one way and end up with multiple income streams.

Diversifying your income in this way not only is smart and helps you spread the risk from having all your eggs in one basket but it also speeds up the journey to going full time.

I learned this lesson the hard way after having most of my income coming from one source in the early days but after a bit of a bad experience began to diversify my income streams (**read about that here**) – it was one of the best things I ever did!

Today I make money from around 12 different streams.

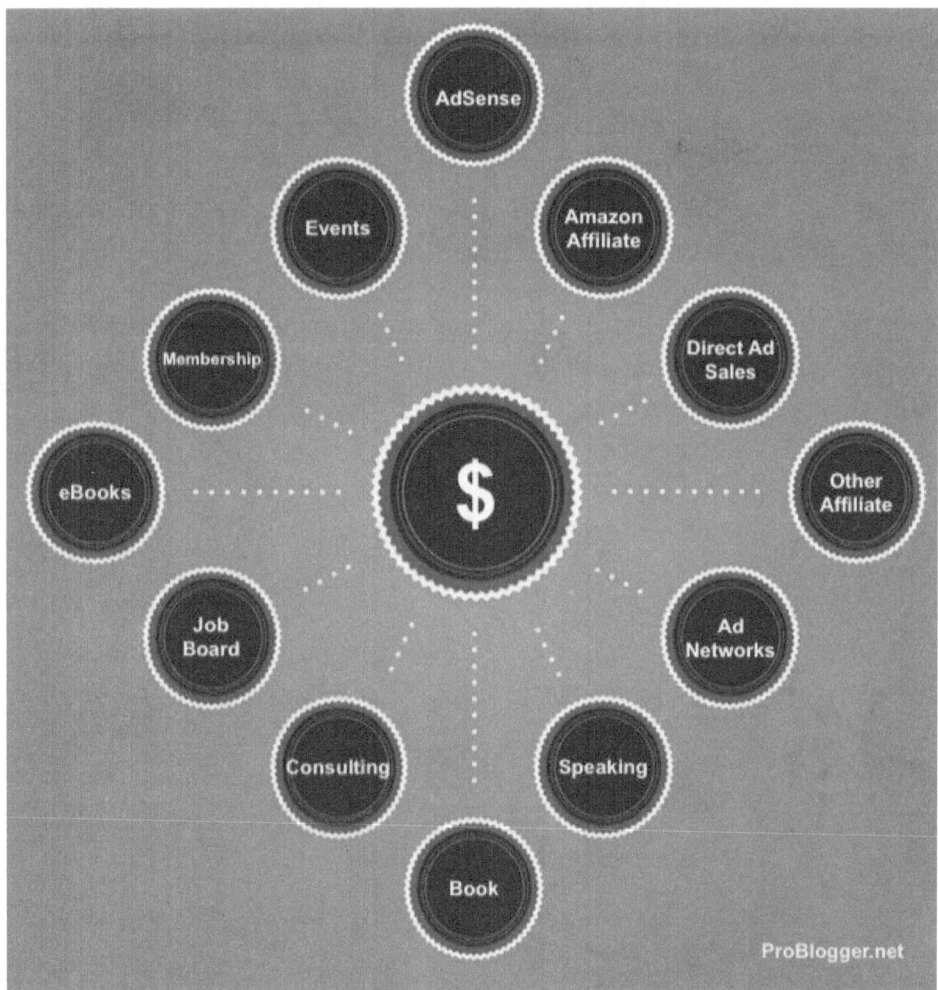

This didn't just happen overnight though – **read about how I added them one at a time here**.

Update: I more recently reported on **how I made money blogging in this income report**.

Direct or Indirect Income?

One last little distinction in terms of income streams.... Some bloggers make money directly 'from' their blog while others make money indirectly 'because' of their blog.

Direct Income – when I started making money from my blogs it was through 'direct' income streams. I put AdSense ads on my blog and promoted some products on Amazon as an affiliate and the more readers I had the more income began to trickle in (it really was a trickle at first). In time as my traffic grew this income grew and I was also able to experiment with other direct forms of income such as selling advertising directly to advertisers.

Indirect Income – later on in my blogging journey opportunity has come for 'indirect' income streams. As my blogs and profile grew as a result of my blogging I was able to sell my services as a speaker and consultant and was offered the opportunity to author a book with the publisher Wiley. Later I was able to start an event for bloggers which also made money. None of this income came directly from the blog – but rather it came 'because' of my blog.

While the way that I make money blogging is a combination of direct and indirect income many bloggers focus upon one or the other.

4. HOW TO MAKE MONEY ON YOU TUBE

You don't need thousands of subscribers to make money on YouTube. Learn the income sources that make real money.

2018 was supposed to be the year of video for many bloggers, the year we start making money on YouTube and other video sharing sites.

Then YouTube threw up a big middle finger to small channels with less than 1,000 subscribers, making it harder to make money.

But is the change in YouTube's advertising policy really an issue? Should the fact that you won't be able to run ads on your videos keep you from making money on the world's second most popular search engine?

Let's look at how much money people make on YouTube, from the YouTube celebrities to smaller channels like you and me. Then I'll show you how to make money on YouTube regardless of how many subscribers you have, income sources for your videos that will make many times over what YouTube ads pay.

What Happened with the YouTube Advertising Change?

So if you haven't been active on YouTube yet, you might not have heard about the new change in advertising policy. It all started in 2017 when advertisers complained about ads being shown on racist and low-quality videos.

Protecting the money rather than its video creators, YouTube instituted a policy that channels would need 10,000 lifetime views before they could make money on ads embedded in the videos.

It didn't help.

Complaints kept coming in from advertisers of low-quality videos and questionable channels so YouTube drastically increased the requirements starting this year.

Video creators now need 1,000 subscribers and at least 4,000 hours of watch time over a 12-month period. Both of these are extremely high hurdles.

I've analyzed over 200 YouTube channels and found creators with less than 1,000 subs get an average of three to five subscribers for every video uploaded. That means between 200 and 300 videos before you're likely to reach enough subscribers to qualify to make money on your videos.

Even YouTube channels with 1,000 subs are being kicked out of the program because of the 4,000-hour requirement. If the average watch time per video is around three minutes, you need a constant stream of videos and new views to hit that 240,000 minutes each year to stay in the program.

Taking all this together, can you still make money on YouTube…even if you're a small niche channel?

How Much Money Does YouTube Pay You for Advertising?

To see why I could care less about the change in YouTube's advertising policy and how to make money on your videos, you have to start with how much YouTube pays for ads.

How to Make More Money on YouTube

Most bloggers start making money with Google Adsense on their blogs. The pay sucks, averaging between $0.006 and $0.015 per page view, but it's quick and easy.

YouTube ad rates are even worse.

YouTube shares 55% of its ad revenue with video creators and books an average of $7.60 per 1,000 ad views. That means you get about $4.18 for every 1,000 views of ads shown on your videos.

That's just $0.0042 per view and doesn't even count if someone clicks off the ad before a certain time has passed.

Worse still is that average of how much YouTube pays on ads isn't the same across all channels. All channels are NOT created equal in the eyes of YouTube!

I researched 24 channels on the platform, watching their "How Much I Make on YouTube" videos. I pulled out their views and ad income then noted the channel topic. What I found is a huge difference in how much some YouTubers make compared to others.

I put the video below together explaining how much YouTube pays and how advertising isn't your best source for income on the platform. I also share five hacks to make more money with YouTube ads.

Does YouTube Discriminate Channels on Pay per View?

Average Ad Revenue per View for 24 Channels

Channel	Niche	Pay	Views	$ per View
Reezy Resells	Amazon Biz	$8,851.77	789,252	$0.01122
Let's Talk Money!	Money	$29,803.01	2,700,000	$0.01104
Graham Stephan	Entrepreneurship	$26,057.41	2,460,777	$0.01059
Wealth Hacker Jeff Rose	Money	$75,149.41	8,569,819	$0.00877
Maryjane Byarm	travel vlog	$13,871.78	2,600,000	$0.00534
Jaskinho	Suspense	$6,167.99	1,302,016	$0.00474
DavidVlasBusiness	Entrepreneurship	$3,672.74	781,886	$0.00470
Vanessa Lau	Entrepreneurship	$7,705.54	1,896,460	$0.00406
Reyes the Entrepreneur	Entrepreneurship	$6,867.42	1,825,806	$0.00376
John Hicks	Bikes vlog	$39,371.19	10,909,946	$0.00361
Jaime Ibanez	Money	$2,842.22	842,463	$0.00337
TipsNNTricks	Hacks	$4,992.42	1,600,000	$0.00312
Dr Jake's Very British Reviews	Lego	$2,401.00	932,235	$0.00258
lotsofgames	gaming	$2,620.08	1,100,000	$0.00238
Damian Keyes	Music biz	$740.89	345,652	$0.00214
Yak Motley	vlog	$22,216.86	10,400,000	$0.00214
Success Insider	Entrepreneurship	$18,453.00	9,199,049	$0.00201
Matt Taylor Variety	vlog	$1,963.46	1,005,528	$0.00195
vanburen20	gaming	$2,003.20	1,362,169	$0.00147
Kings Must Rise	Cars	$1,339.11	940,400	$0.00142
Youtube Shortcuts	YouTube	$1,784.10	1,254,811	$0.00142
AutoVlog	Cars	$7,823.45	6,473,503	$0.00121
Copper Creek Cuts Lawn Care	landscaping	$1,415.85	1,200,000	$0.00118
Austin Campbell	Cars	$3,805.45	12,912,244	$0.00029
		Average $ per View		$0.00394
		Median $ per View		$0.00285

How Much Does YouTube Pay per View?

You can see that finance and entrepreneurship channels can do really well, with YouTube paying upwards of a penny per view on videos. Vlogs, gaming and lifestyle channels don't do nearly as well with an average closer to $2 per 1,000 video views.

I know it's a lot of numbers but stick with me for a second to see just how crappy a deal this is.

If you publish two videos a week and get an average of 500 views on each, an extremely ambitious goal, you'd still make less than $20 a month.

If you publish two videos a week and get an average of 500 views on each, an extremely ambitious goal for a small YouTube channel, you'd still make less than $20 a month on the best rates.

DON'T CLICK OUT IN FRUSTRATION!

Before you throw your hands up and give-up, You can make money on YouTube. I'm showing you this ad income not to frustrate your YouTube channel goals but to prove that you need to be focusing on other income sources to make real money on the platform. Let's look at some famous examples of YouTubers making big bank and then I'll show you how to make the real bucks.

Want my three favorite strategies for growing a YouTube channel? I'm doing a free webinar on growing subscribers fast and growing your channel into a legit business that reaches millions. I've reached over 3.5 million people with my channel and these are the three tricks that helped me most.

Space is limited on the webinar so click through and reserve your spot here!

How Much Do Famous YouTube Celebrities Make?

Everyone gets pulled into the myth of making money on YouTube by the millions made by a very few YouTube stars. Exact income isn't always shared but estimates are pretty easy to come by with the top ten all making more than $10 million a year and thousands of dollars every time they upload a video.

Six-year old Ryan of 'Ryan's Toy Review' is estimated to make $11 million by opening and playing with toys in videos for his 10 million subscribers. I think my 5-year old son is responsible for about half of the views on the channel. Ryan and his parents have been masterful at finding different revenue streams from his own line of toys to licensing and a contract with Nickelodeon.

Daniel Middleton is estimated to have made $16.5 million by playing Minecraft in videos for his 18 million subscribers.

But think about those numbers. NBC gets about 18 million viewers for its Sunday Night Football broadcasts, the #1 rated show on TV. If the show was on YouTube, it would make just $1.2 million for the 17-game season…

YouTube celebrities are getting millions of views on each video and making a fraction of what is being paid on traditional media. You have to reach nearly 12 MILLION PEOPLE a year with your videos just to make YouTube a full-time job based on what you make with ads.

How to Make Money on YouTube – the Real Way

Making money blogging or on YouTube has never been about selling advertising space. I'm always amazed when I read a blog post and have to scroll through four ad blocks within the content. It's so annoying and how much is that blogger really making off the ads?

Making real money has always been about finding the income sources that pay more, the income strategies that don't depend on millions of monthly views.

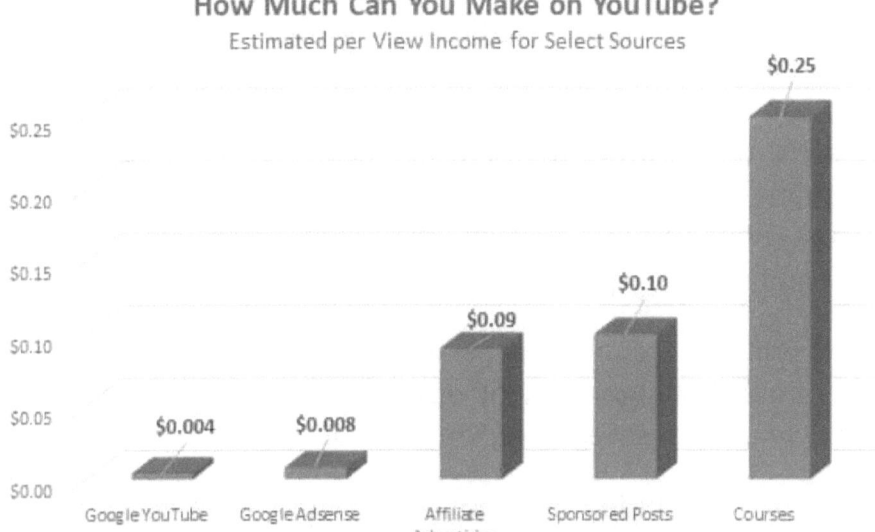

How Much Can You Make on YouTube?

Estimated per View Income for Select Sources

Source: Blogger estimates based on 2018 blogger survey

How to Make Money on YouTube Every Month

It's no different in making money on YouTube. Not only will finding the best income sources help you make more per view, integrating a few of these into your content strategy will help diversify your income so you make a consistent paycheck every month.

3 Ways to Make Money on YouTube

Affiliate advertising is a good start but still not the best income source for bloggers and video creators. I make an average of $0.09 per page view from affiliates, that's from people clicking through to an affiliate and then signing up for the service.

Sure, it's harder to get an affiliate commission than it is to simply get someone to click on an ad but the payout is much higher.

Making money with affiliates on YouTube works the same way it does with a blog.

- Find three or four affiliates that speak directly to your target audience, that solve a common problem.
- Create a video reviewing the service and how it helps users or integrate the affiliates into your YouTube video ideas
- Create a demonstration video specifically for your audience
- Interview other users of the affiliate
- Copy your affiliate link in the description to the video, preferably within the first few lines

Sponsored videos are another way to monetize your YouTube channel without having to rely on embedded ads. Again, this works the same way as sponsored posts on your blog.

Talking with other video creators, I've found an average rate of between $0.05 and $0.15 per view for sponsored videos. So if you get an average of 500 views each video, you can charge a sponsor about $50 to mention them during the video.

That's more than 20-times what you'd make from YouTube advertising! You can make even more if you're able to prove your YouTube video promotion strategy to sponsors.

The final way to make money on YouTube, and this should be your goal in blogging as well, is to create your own courses and products. Any time you remove the advertiser and connect directly with your viewers for your own products, you are going to make more money.

This means quick products like self-publishing and printables as well as the higher-value products like video courses. If you can convert just one viewer in every 1,000 views to your $250 video course, you'll have made $0.25 per view…more than 59-times what you would make with YouTube ads.

Ultimately, a lot of how much you make on YouTube comes down to your channel growth. Growing subscribers and growing your income are inextricably linked so you need to look for ways to grow on YouTube if you want to make more money.

In this video, I detail three strategies I used to grow my community from zero to over 75,000 subscribers in less than 18 months!

How Much Money Can You Make on YouTube?

So answering the question here, I hope you understand now that you can make A LOT OF MONEY on YouTube even with a small channel.

We didn't talk much about growing subscribers on YouTube in this post because I wanted to keep it about making money and it's less about your sub count than you might think. It's not so much the size of your channel but how engaged you community is and the product strategies you're using.

For example, I just did a collab with a YouTube creator that has just 15,000 subscribers but has managed to make over $18,000 over the last year with products, affiliates, sponsorships and ads...I've also seen channels with hundreds of thousands of subscribers barely making enough to cover their editing costs.

As a rule of thumb, I've found a good goal to reach for is to make your subscriber count in dollars annually. I don't know why it works but the numbers just seem to come out. Every time I look at how much a channel has made over the last year, the ones actively trying to make money anyway, it very often seems to be close to their subscriber count.

Of course, this isn't a hard-rule and you aren't a failure if you're making less than your sub-count. It's just a good place to start when trying to make money on YouTube.

If you're serious about growing a YouTube channel and making this a legit business, click through and check out **Crushing YouTube**. Get every secret I used to grow my YouTube channel from zero to 75,000 subscribers in less than 18 months!

Get Your Copy of Crushing YouTube on Kindle or Paperback

Making money on YouTube doesn't have to depend on advertising and it certainly doesn't mean being held back by new YouTube advertiser policies. Stop being restricted by how much YouTube pays on ads! Learn how to make real money with your videos by using the income sources that make more money per view.

5 HOW TO MAKE MONEY ON FACEBOOK

You can how to earn money online from facebook in various ways. One of such ways is to sell a certain number of likes with a price tag.

You can be get paid for selling facebook page likes. But this way you will not always earn the same amount as it is shown here. I have seen people selling 1000 likes in Rs.50. Your earning depends on the demography you are targeting and type of client you can get.

There are certainly other ways to make money on facebook by which you can earn much better amount. Although some of them require initial investment either monetary or time but you will get a lot of money in return.

#1. Earn money through facebook page

A facebook page has the potential to earn as much as a billion. The Indian startup Inshort was first started as a facebook page which later became a startup for sharing any news article in 60 words.

To earn money from a facebook fan page, first you must create one. And then follow this small guide.

How to earn money from facebook page

Step-1: Find a niche

You must be clear from day one that you have to make money from your fb page. For that, you must know the potential of a niche which will help you to earn money and your interest in the topic.

For example, an affiliate marketing fan page will generate a decent earning from websites like amazon.

Earning from a facebook page is not a fortnight work. It is also important that you must have the basic knowledge about the field so that you can create content for your fans and inspire other people to like your page.

Step-2: Publish content on your facebook page

Start sharing content. Your content should be such that people read/watch and share.

Facebook pages are said to have a low organic reach and people often forget you if you are not consistent.

You must have a pre-written pool of content. Also, you should schedule your posts so that if you are busy somewhere, your page will still keep running.

You can schedule your social media posts with apps like Buffer and HootSuite.

Step-3: Make relationship

In marketing relationship building is compulsory. You will get your first payment from collaborative promotions or as sponsored posts. Sponsored post means that you get paid to write (and post) about a brand, on your fb page.

Or, you can make money by posting links of other brands.

(Check – Best credit card in India)

Step-4: Make more money

If you have a decent fan base and have developed a name in the town, you can apply to the affiliate programs to earn more money. Few famous affiliate providers are clickbank, cj, shareasale, amazon etc.

#2. Sell products on Facebook to make money

You can use facebook's **make an offer** feature to earn money by selling products.

Put the link of your product in the link box and give a coupon code to offer a discount on the product.

You can also use an affiliate link from any e-commerce site and attach a coupon code (not necessary if the company does not offer a discount). Your fans will buy the product from your link and you will earn money through the affiliate.

You can put the paid links on facebook from any of the websites, Amazon, Flipkart, Snapdeal, or whichever provides a commission on their earning.

Earn more on offers by promoting on facebook:

-

- o Give an attractive offer like 10-15% discount or buy one get one free. Your offer should be competitive or better than your competitors.

-
  - o Promote this offer with facebook paid ads.

- Or, involve influential facebook pages or people to promote your offer.

#3. Freelance facebook marketer earns well

You can earn $50 per hour by becoming a freelance facebook marketer.

The skills required to become a freelance facebook marketer are:

-
  - o Analyse facebook stats. You must be able to predict with data analysis that, which type of posts work better on which day of the week. Marketing can become successful only if we are able to measure the stats. Like google has their analytics for websites, facebook has its own analytics for pages.
  - o Ability to make marketing strategies and decisions. A marketing campaign cannot be successful without a strategic planning. An effective marketer knows what will be the results of a campaign at the end of the month.

- Ability to create a facebook friendly content. For example, posts with 40 characters on facebook get 86% more engagement. You must know which type of content works better in a situation.

Other ways to make money on facebook

#4. Become influencer

You can also earn money becoming an influencer with your normal profile. If posts on your facebook wall get decent likes and comments, becoming an influencer is a good way to earn money.

Also if you have a fan following and you interact with them through your personal profile, then you can make money by signing up through an influencer account on blogmint.com or fromote.com to start earning.

After signing up, you will be required to fill a form where you will enter your profile information and you can fix price as an influencer. For example, you may charge 5,000 per facebook post giving emphasis to a brand.

#5. Earn money through facebook apps

You can earn money by becoming a facebook app developer. Or, you can develop a facebook app independently. In your app you can earn money by applying for banner ads or you can sell virtual goods of your own or from some gaming companies like EA, Zynga, Popcap etc.

#6. Earn money by account selling

You can earn money by selling your old facebook accounts. Earlier it had become a trend to make more than one account. But now marketers are buying those accounts for their promotional purpose as facebook gives more weightage to an old account.

Similarly, you can sell your old facebook group or page with a good number of fan base.

#7. Earn money from facebook group

You can make a facebook group. Try to make a group with more than 10k members and a good engagement in conversation around a niche. Keep the members engaged with relevant questions, blog posts, images, polls etc.

You can earn money on facebook group by,

- o Paid surveys

- o Sponsored content.

- o Selling your own product/book/services.

- Affiliate marketing.

Over to you

Making money from facebook is a little tricky. Facebook does not allow organic promotion to a large number of fans. But the trick here is, if you can keep your audiences engaged, you can win the organic reach to a much larger extent.

You can suggest me more earning methods from facebook here in the comments.

To conclude :

Perfecting product quality has numerous benefits for any company. The positive correlation between product quality and sales should be reason enough to make quality a top priority in a business strategy. The trust, credibility, and loyalty that comes from happy customers builds repeat sales and ignites positive recommendations about a product that helps a company reach new audiences.

TABLE OF CONTENTS

www.ingramcontent.com/pod-product-compliance
Lightning Source LLC
Chambersburg PA
CBHW020619220526
45463CB00006B/2625